On the WING

North American Birds 2

Andrea Voon

Richard Han

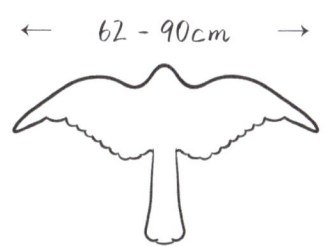

62 - 90cm

Cooper's Hawk

French: Épervier de Cooper

Little wings, little wings, flap flap flap...

Undercover agents in the forests are on the wing.

Cooper's Hawks, Cooper's Hawks, clap clap clap...

Skillfully hunt and kill prey on the wing.

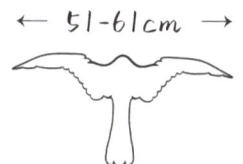

← 51-61cm →

American Kestrel

French: Crécerelle d'Amérique

Little wings, little wings, flap flap flap…

Sportscasters in the grasslands are on the wing.

American Kestrels, American Kestrels, clap clap clap…

Scan and dive for prey on the wing.

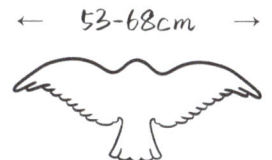

53-68cm

Merlin

French: Faucon émerillon

Little wings, little wings, flap flap flap…

Helicopter pilots in the forests are on the wing.

Merlins, Merlins, clap clap clap…

Forage low, and chase some birds on the wing.

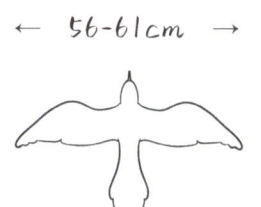

$\leftarrow$ 56-61cm $\rightarrow$

Black-billed Magpie

French: Pie d'Amérique

Little wings, little wings, flap flap flap...

Veterinarians in the open woodlands are on the wing.

Black-billed Magpies, Black-billed Magpies, clap clap clap...

Pick ticks from elks and deers on the wing.

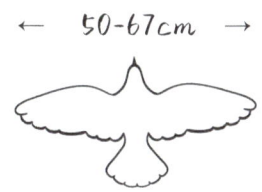

← 50-67cm →

Rock Pigeon

French: Pigeon biset

Little wings, little wings, flap flap flap…

Postmen in the towns are on the wing.

Rock Pigeons, Rock Pigeons, clap clap clap…

Follow the sun for navigation on the wing.

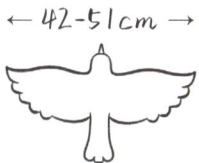

← 42-51 cm →

Northern Flicker

French: Pic flamboyant

Little wings, little wings, flap flap flap...

Doctors in the open woodlands are on the wing.

Northern Flickers, Northern Flickers, clap clap clap...

Peck on sick tree branches on the wing.

California Quail

French: Colin de Californie

Little wings, little wings, flap flap flap…

Choir singers in the scrubs are on the wing.

California Quails, California Quails, clap clap clap…

Gather moisture from bugs and seeds on the wing.

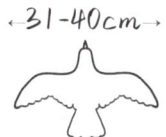

European Starling

French: Étourneau sansonnet

Little wings, little wings, flap flap flap...

Dance groups in the towns are on the wing.

European Starlings, European Starlings, clap clap clap...

Perform a stunning murmuration on the wing.

Tree Swallow

French: Hirondelle bicolore

30-35cm

Little wings, little wings, flap flap flap...

Air forces at the lakes and ponds are on the wing.

Tree Swallows, Tree Swallows, clap clap clap...

Dive-bomb predators on the wing.

Western Tanager

French: Piranga à tête rouge

Little wings, little wings, flap flap flap…

Firefighters in the forests are on the wing.

Western Tanagers, Western Tanagers, clap clap clap…

Look like a flickering flame on the wing.

← 29cm →

.12cm.

Anna's Hummingbird

French: Colibri d'Anna

Tiny wings, tiny wings, flap flap flap…

Magicians in the open woodlands are on the wing.

Anna's Hummingbirds, Anna's Hummingbirds, clap clap clap…

Change colors every second on the wing.

-11cm-

Rufous Hummingbird

French: Colibri roux

Tiny wings, tiny wings, flap flap flap…

Gardeners in the open woodlands are on the wing.

Rufous Hummingbirds, Rufous Hummingbirds, clap clap clap…

Somersault and collect pollens on the wing.

Little wings, tiny wings, flap flap flap…

Ready for an adventure on the wing.

Little wings, tiny wings, clap clap clap…

Our EARTH is full of life on the wing.

28

Author

Andrea Voon

Over the past few years, Andrea has learned and grown with her family as a full-time mother in Canada. Back in Malaysia, she was a Chinese immersion elementary school teacher. In 2021, Andrea started her journey as an author. Growing up in a multilingual environment, Andrea loves the beauty of languages on their own. She has the vision to publish picture books to support bilingual families in raising their children in English, Chinese, and Cantonese reading.

Photographer

Richard Han

Richard loves to practice patience through his lenses of the natural world. He enjoys observing the wildlife and photographing the natural lifestyles that animals live. He is excited to present the beautiful photos that he captured in dreamy tones and colors to all the birds lover.

Check out more books by Andrea Voon.

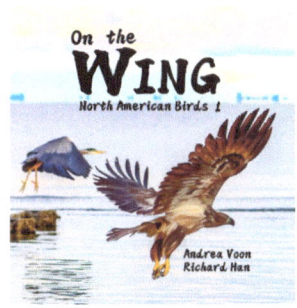
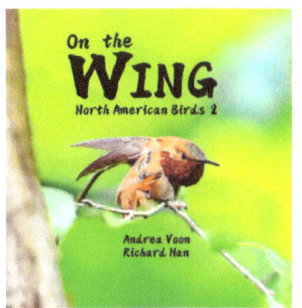
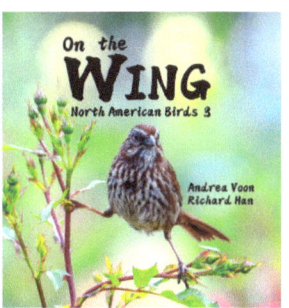
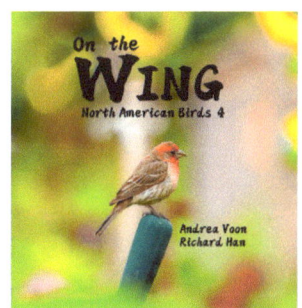

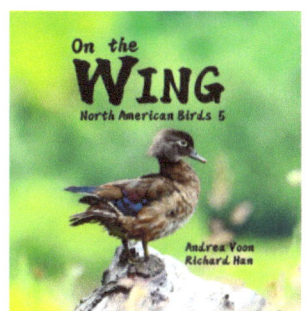

To **Shirley Han, Derek, Eliana, Alayna & Magnus Dominus**

with love -- Andrea. V

For **Richard Han**
The patience in natural photography

ISBN 978-1-998856-46-6
Text Copyright © 2024 Andrea Voon
Photo Credit © 2024 Richard Han

www.ingramcontent.com/pod-product-compliance
Lightning Source LLC
Chambersburg PA
CBHW041623120626
46551CB00003B/555